To
_____

From
_____

Date
_____

Message
_____

DEVOTIONS OF COMFORT AND GRACE by Earl Allen

© 1999 Christian Art Gifts, RSA

Copyright © 1983 by Earl Allen. Originally published under the title *Devotionals for Times of Sorrow* by Baker Books, a division of Baker Book House Company, Grand Rapids, Michigan, 49516, USA. All rights reserved.

First edition 1999
Second edition 2006

Designed by Christian Art Gifts

Scripture taken from the *Holy Bible*, King James Version. Copyright © 1962 by The Zondervan Corporation. Used by permission.

Scripture taken from the *Holy Bible*, New International Version®. Copyright © 1973, 1978, 1984 by the International Bible Society. Used by permission of Zondervan Publishing House. All rights reserved.

Printed in China

ISBN-10: 1-86920-595-2
ISBN-13: 978-1-86920-595-9

06 07 08 09 10 11 12 13 14 15 – 13 12 11 10 9 8 7 6 5 4

DEVOTIONS
of COMFORT
and
GRACE

R. EARL ALLEN

christian
art gifts.

The Christian's comfort

Fear thou not; for I am with thee: be not dismayed;
for I am thy God: I will strengthen thee; yeah,
I will help thee; yea, I will uphold thee
with the right hand of my righteousness.

ISAIAH 41:10

Nothing stuns us as deeply as the death of some-one close. Losing a loved one is at first a severe shock; we feel almost out of touch with reality. The tragedy and finality of our loss overwhelms us with loneliness. Later, we realize that our future holds many difficult changes and choices.

Though your loss may feel very painful right now, God has promised to be with you and com-fort you. The prophet Isaiah writes, "As one whom his mother comforteth, so will I [God] comfort you" (Isa. 66:13). These words were given to Is-rael long ago, but the tender promise speaks to us still. God usually answers the desperate "why?" of His people with the assurance, "I am near; I will comfort you."

Tryon Edwards tells of a wise man who went

to someone in sorrow and said, "I did not come to comfort you; God only can do that. But I did come to say how deeply and tenderly I feel for you in your affliction." Caring individuals cannot of themselves bring comfort that truly satisfies a bereaved heart, but God can use them to minister the comfort He provides.

When you are suffering because of the death of a loved one, you can receive encouragement from the Scriptures and insights from others who have gone through a similar experience. As you quietly trust God day by day, He will bestow solace like spring showers in the desert.

> The soft, sweet summer was warm and glowing;
> Bright were the blossoms on every bough;
> I trusted Him when the roses were blooming –
> I trust Him now.
> – Anonymous –

Lord, please comfort me as only You can. Bring healing to my aching heart and place hope before my tearful eyes. In Jesus' name. Amen.

A glimpse of heaven

Therefore are they before the throne of God,
and serve him day and night in his temple:
and he that sitteth on the throne shall dwell
among them. They shall hunger no more,
neither thirst any more; ... For the Lamb which
is in the midst of the throne shall feed them, and
shall lead them unto living fountains of waters:
and God shall wipe away all tears from their eyes.

REVELATION 7:15-17

If we could catch the smallest glimpse of heaven,
we would not weep for the dead, but would ask
them to weep for us. So magnificent is God's eternal provision for those who have trusted Him that
we cannot comprehend the happiness they enjoy
in His presence.

In the Book of Revelation the apostle John gives
us several glimpses of heaven. Those saints who
have died and been lifted above this world's tribulations are given divine comfort by Him "that sitteth
on the throne." They are fed in green pastures and
led to the fountains of living waters by the Good

Shepherd. Jesus Himself wipes the tears from their eyes. If only we could comprehend their joy in that heavenly land, perhaps we could better accept the solace God offers us while we remain behind.

Jesus promised that after He returned to the Father He would send "another Comforter" who would remain with us forever. The word *another* means "another of the same kind." This other Comforter is the Holy Spirit, and it is His mission on earth to guide and comfort us the same way that Jesus Christ does those who dwell with Him above. Knowing that our loved ones are surrounded with all the glories of heaven gives us reason to rejoice in God's blessings as we work out our earthly lives.

> There is a land where everlasting suns shed everlasting brightness; where the soul drinks from the living streams of love that roll by God's high throne … O how blest to look from this dark prison to that shrine, to inhale one breath of Paradise divine, and enter into that eternal rest which waits the Sons of God!
>
> – John Bowring –

Heavenly Father, grant all of us who sorrow the comfort of the Holy Spirit. In Jesus' name. Amen.

Fear not death

———— ⟳ ————

For to me to live is Christ, and to die is gain.
PHILIPPIANS 1:21

An old proverb says, "What death is to a caterpillar, to God is a butterfly." Fulfillment of life comes only by passing through death. The writer of Hebrews says, "It is appointed unto men once to die" (9:27). If God has purposed that all should die, there must be something good in God's intention, because God is good.

When the apostle Paul wrote the Philippian letter, he sat in a Roman jail awaiting martyrdom. Many of God's purposes had been realized in his life, and he felt sure that through his death God would be glorified even more. So he wrote a startling phrase which is contrary to all human thinking: "to die is gain."

For those who believe in Jesus Christ, death means being transported to a higher dimension of life. We need not fear death for ourselves or for those we have placed in the grave. They are lost to us, but the resurrection of Jesus Christ assures us that their life blossoms into eternal glory.

Death brings to completion the salvation of man. Our initial faith in Jesus Christ frees us from the penalty of sin. Growth and maturity in the Christian life remove us from the power of sin, but only death and resurrection release us from the presence of sin. If we would receive God's effective comfort in our sorrow, we need to comprehend something of His wonderful purpose. God's omnipotence tames even dreadful death to be His useful servant for good to those who love Him. Because on the other side we become the perfected creatures He intended, even death is gain.

> Life is a journey, not a home; a road, not a city of habitation; and the enjoyments and blessings we have are but little inns on the roadside of life, where we may be refreshed for a moment, that with new strength we may push on … to the rest that remaineth for the people of God.
>
> – Anonymous –

Father, thank You for making death a doorway to victory. Comfort us with the assurance that our loss is gain for You and for those who are with You. Amen.

The light of the world

*Every good gift and every perfect gift is from above,
and cometh down from the Father of lights, with
whom is no variableness, neither shadow of turning.*

JAMES 1:17

A blind woman strides along toward her office, swinging her white cane before her as she crosses a wide, busy street.

At a committee meeting she records the minutes in braille, clicking along faster than many sighted people write longhand, then turns the page over and reads it aloud easily.

Like this woman, we too are blind. Without God we grope in spiritual darkness. However, unlike this woman, we have not learned to cope with our darkness, for the aids we adopt to help us "see" are ineffective and only perpetuate our spiritual blindness.

The apostle John, speaking of Jesus Christ in his Gospel, declares, "That was the true Light, which lighteth every man that cometh into the world" (1:9). When our way is uncertain and our decisions are difficult, we can gain spiritual perception only by living close to Christ.

Notice that James calls God the "Father of lights." God's unchanging love radiates blessings toward us at all times. Just as the sun's rays bathe the earth, so God's rays of concern envelop us. He is aware of the hazards of life that we do not see, and maintains a continual vigil over us.

I asked the flowers as they grew
Richer and lovelier in their hue,
"What makes your life so pure and bright?"
They answered, "Looking toward the light."
"Ah, secret clear!" said heart of mine.
"God meant my life to be like thine,
Richer, heavenlier, and more bright,
By simply looking toward the Light."
– Myron Lee Pontius –

Heavenly Father, help me to walk boldly and wisely in the light You shed on my pathway. Amen.

Not cloudless days;
not rose-strewn ways;
not care-free years,
devoid of sorrow's tears –
but strength to bear
your load of human care,
and grace to live aright
and keep your raiment white,
and love to see you through;
that is God's pledge to you.

— ANONYMOUS —

I lift up my eyes to the hills –
where does my help come from?
My help comes from the LORD,
the Maker of heaven and earth.

– PSALM 121:1-2, NIV –

Precious tears

———— ⟨ℓℓℓ⟩ ————

Thou tellest my wanderings: put thou my tears
into thy bottle: are they not in thy book? When
I cry unto thee, then shall mine enemies turn
back: this I know; for God is for me.
PSALM 56:8-9

In sorrow tears flow frequently. The Creator who made us and knows our needs gave us tears as an outlet for sadness. Leigh Hunt has said, "Tears hinder sorrow from becoming despair." If we do not weep outwardly, we are torn inwardly.

Tears do not flow only from the pitiful and the weak; they spring also from the love and tenderness of the strong. We should never be ashamed of our tears, whether in private sorrow or public grieving. They speak for us of love toward those we have lost. Tears alleviate our grief and encourage the healing of our wounds.

It is comforting to realize that God notices our tears. The psalmist said, "Put thou my tears into thy bottle: are they not in thy book?" God records our tears in His book of remembrance, as though

14

He were saying. "I have seen your sorrow and I have provided comfort that is greater than your grief."

When we cry to God, the psalmist said, our enemies are turned back. In time of grief our biggest enemies are those things that afflict our minds and torment our emotions. God protects us from these foes by relieving our despair, confusion, and fear. He assuages our sorrow with His peace and joy.

> There is sacredness in tears. They are not the marks of weakness, but of power. They speak more eloquently than ten thousand tongues. They are the messengers of overwhelming grief, of deep contrition, and of unspeakable love.
> – Washington Irving –

Father, thank You for noticing our tears and hearing our cries. In our weakness, Lord, be our strength. Amen.

Resurrection

─── ⟨⟨⟨~ ───

Jesus said unto her, "I am the resurrection, and the life: he that believeth in me, though he were dead, yet shall he live: And whosoever liveth and believeth in me shall never die. Believest thou this?"

JOHN 11:25-26

How blessed we would be if only we could comprehend the eternal fellowship we will have with Jesus Christ! For this is the full meaning of the resurrection; because of this we can hope in spite of our sorrow.

Some day in the future the trumpet of the Lord will sound; then those who believe and are alive at that time will be united with their Lord and with all the saints who have died. This is the promise of God. Only such an event could fulfill that nature of Jesus Christ, who claimed, "I am the resurrection and the life."

The light of this hope should shine perpetually in the eyes of every Christian. No darkness should dispel the glorious image of our resurrected Lord.

The apostle Paul said, "But I would not have

you to be ignorant, brethren, concerning them which are asleep, that ye sorrow not, even as others which have no hope" (1 Thess. 4:13). In the death of another believer, or in the approach of our own death, we can be comforted by this blessed assurance from our Lord: "Whosoever liveth and believeth in Me shall never die."

It is recovery and not death. Blessed are they that sleep in the Lord; his life is hidden in Christ. In his Redeemer's life it is hidden, and in His glory will it be disclosed.
– Samuel Taylor Coleridge, *speaking of a dear friend's death* –

Thank You, heavenly Father, for the promise of resurrection. Help me to live in that hope. Amen.

A pathway to beauty

It is good for me that I have been afflicted;
that I might learn thy statutes.
PSALM 119:71

Who of us in the midst of trouble or sorrow does not ask why he is afflicted? Yet most of us in response to this question consider only the negative possibilities; we cannot resist the tendency to presume that our afflictions are punishment for our character or our behavior. How this veils the face of our loving God and dims His light from view!

The truth is that adversity and affliction come upon the righteous as well as the unrighteous. However, the Bible assures us that the righteous who live by faith will receive God's deliverance.

Our comprehension of God's purposes is so incomplete, so infinitesimal compared to God's overview. God's omnipotence enables Him to bring forth good from things pleasant and unpleasant. From this side of eternity we have no way of judging the beauty and worth of what God is producing.

While traveling recently, I passed a roadside stand where an artist was selling his paintings. All were painted in the brightest colors on black velvet. The images seemed to jump out from their dark background. The light metallic hues would have been lost on white canvas. Without the dark background there would have been no beauty.

Perhaps we mistakenly think that God has to use white canvas, and therefore we wonder if He exists in the blackness that surrounds us. However, it is impossible for us, knowing only part of God's purpose, to judge His ways. Simply look at the beauty, order, and wonder of the universe, and let the Artist paint as He will.

No affliction would trouble a child of God,
if he knew God's reasons for sending it.
– James Henry Morgan –

Lord, I trust You to bring beauty from this, too; give me patience to see it in Your time. Amen.

The greatest change

So when this corruptible shall have put on incorruption, and this mortal shall have put on immortality, then shall be brought to pass the saying that is written, Death is swallowed up in victory.
1 CORINTHIANS 15:54

We fear change, especially the greatest change of all – death. Change pulls us into areas of the unknown. That makes us fearful, but it also challenges us. If we trust God we can be thankful for the wonderful changes He brings about, even through death.

Michael Faraday, the famous scientist, teacher, and inventor, believed in the resurrection of the body. One day he was distressed to hear a group of students sneering at the idea. He asked them to gather around his lab table; as they watched he threw a silver cup into sulphuric acid, dissolving the metal. He then added common salt to precipitate the silver, and with it he fashioned a new cup.

"Look!" he said. "If I, an ordinary scientist, can dissolve a cup and then remake it more beautiful than before, why think it incredible that God can restore in resurrection glory the bodies which have been dissolved by death?"

Christ by His resurrection has conquered death and assured those who follow Him of a similar triumph. Because Christ has risen we need no longer fear change; the unknown holds no threat, only promise. Paul's words "we shall all be changed" and "death is swallowed up in victory" give us assurance. Because of Jesus Christ we can rejoice at the homegoing of a loved one who belongs to Him.

The body of Benjamin Franklin (like the cover of an old book, its contents torn out, and stript of its lettering and gilding) lies here, food for worms; yet the work itself shall not be lost, for it will, as he believed, appear once more, in a new and more beautiful edition, corrected and amended by the Author.

– Benjamin Franklin, *his own epitaph* –

As we have accepted Your promises, Lord Jesus, we anticipate the glory of living in eternity with You. Amen.

*Silence is no certain token
that no secret grief is there.
Sorrow which is never spoken
is the heaviest load to bear.*

– FRANCES RIDLEY HAVERGAL –

Earth has no sorrow
that heaven cannot heal.

– THOMAS MOORE –

The covering of love

*Herein is love, not that we loved God,
but that he loved us, and sent his Son to
be the propitiation [covering] for our sins.*
1 JOHN 4:10

Love plays a strange role in sorrow. Someone has said that "if all would speak as kindly of the living as in epitaphs they do of the dead, slander and censorious gossip would soon be strangers in the world." There is no hypocrisy in remembering the good and forgetting the bad. Let your memory of your loved one be as fond as you will, for that is the attitude of love.

Might not a painter, planning a picture of a friend who has a blemish in one eye, pose him so that the picture would show only the other side of his face?

Yet in being kind to the dead, often we are too hard on ourselves. No one ever loses a loved one without thinking, "If only I had done this for him," or "If only I hadn't said that to her." Such guilt complicates grief and extends it beyond reasonable limits. If we are able to cover the sins of the departed in this imperfect world, just imagine with what ease they forget our faults as they live in perfected love.

Let us also partake of God's forgiveness. God sent His Son as a sin offering to cover our blemishes from His sight. If we receive this merciful gift of God's love, our sorrows will be less and our peace of mind greater. Love covers a multitude of sins – and our God loves and forgives us.

> Love covers a multitude of sins. When a scar cannot be taken away, the next kind office is to hide it ... It is a noble and great thing to cover the blemishes and to excuse the failings of a friend; to draw a curtain before his stains, and to display his perfections; to bury his weakness in silence, but to proclaim his virtues from the housetop.
> – Robert South –

Father, cover us with Your love in our times of sorrow, and comfort us with the assurance of Your forgiveness. Amen.

Our eternal home

For we know that if our earthly house of this taber-
nacle were dissolved, we have a building of God, an
house not made with hands, eternal in the heavens.
2 CORINTHIANS 5:1

The apostle Paul compares life in this body to living in a tent. Tents are adequate temporary dwell-
ings, but for long-term shelter we want something sturdier and more beautiful. Paul describes
the resurrected body as "an house not made with
hands, eternal in the heavens."

Only when we understand the final and eternal
results of the resurrection do we see death in true
perspective. For when we die we will simply move
out of a tent. And we will no longer experience the
sorrow and grief that are characteristic of living in
these tent-bodies. The mansion God has planned
for our eternal home glows with beauty and rings
with gladness. Thus we may rejoice, for our loved
ones (as will we ourselves someday) experience an
existence in heaven far better than we ever could
imagine in this world.

God wants to give us the greatest gift of all – eternal life with Him. It is His plan that the temporal should give way to the eternal, the tent to a palace, the carnal body to a glorified body. Thus death actually enlarges the dimensions of our existence. As Milton said, "Death is the golden key that opens the palace of eternity."

> They who die in Jesus live in a larger, fuller, nobler life, by the very cessation of care, change, strife, and struggle. Above all, they live a fuller, grander life, because they sleep in Jesus and are gathered into His embrace, and awake with Him, clothed with white robes, awaiting the adoption – to wit, the redemption of the body.
>
> – Alexander Maclaren –

Lord, thank You for conquering death and giving us the brilliant hope of the resurrection. Amen.

The watered valley

*Blessed is the man whose strength
is in thee; in whose heart are the
ways [of God's people]. Who passing
through the valley of Baca make it a well.*

PSALM 84:5-6

In the arid Middle East, wells are essential to life. These Scripture verses, hidden away in a less familiar Psalm, take more meaning from that fact. The Hebrew word *Baca* means "weeping"; therefore the "valley of Baca" is not necessarily a geographical place, but can mean any sorrow through which one must pass. This tear-filled valley becomes a well, however, if we look to God in our time of need and draw from Him strength and comfort to sustain us. To the ancient people this image was vivid and pertinent.

Jesus has provided for us "a well of water springing up into everlasting life." He promised the Samaritan woman at Jacob's well that "whosoever drinketh of the water that I shall give him shall never thirst" (John 4:14).

When we pass through a deep valley of sorrow and weeping, we have a precious opportunity to dig a well that will refresh ourselves and others. As we trust Jesus Christ for our needs we begin to drink of the water He gives. In sorrow we have a tendency to look inward, but introspection threatens to make us despair. Only when we look upward to the Lord do we receive strength to go on.

No one chooses to walk into the valley of weeping – but then, there is usually no choice about sorrow. Let us make the most of it by relying on God the father as our strength, the Holy Spirit as our Comforter, and Jesus Christ, who was dead but is alive forevermore, as our hope.

Be content with your surroundings, but not with yourself until you have made the most of them.
– Anonymous –

Loving Father, please be my strength as I pass through this valley of sorrow. Amen.

Our unchanging God

Jesus Christ the same yesterday,
and today, and for ever.
HEBREWS 13:8

When our faith rests in the eternal God made known to us in Jesus Christ, we can meet life or death with confidence. For Jesus, whom we have made our Lord, called Lazarus from the grave; He met Mary in the garden on Easter morning. He conquered death two thousand years ago and will remain victorious over it forever.

Christ does not change, but we do. We are hindered by our small frame of dust. When illness or accident comes, we realize the frailty of the temporal shell of our bodies. A physical illness, which we have scarcely thought of before, may become a threat to our very existence.

Though we may move from strength to weakness, we can rest assured that our God is always strong. Though we sink from light into darkness, our God is always light. And when we pass from life into death, our God will be there waiting for us. Our changing fortunes are watched over by a loving Father who never grows weary, weak, or inattentive.

"Hast thou not known?" exclaimed Isaiah, "hast thou not heard, that the everlasting God, the LORD, the Creator of the ends of the earth, fainteth not, neither is weary? there is no searching of His understanding" (40:28). Though you may feel weak as you pass through times of sorrow, the everlasting God who loves you is strong.

> It fortifies my soul to know
> That though I perish, truth is so:
> That, howso'er I stray and range,
> Whate'er I do, Thou dost not change.
> I steadier step when I recall
> That, if I slip, Thou dost not fall.
> – Arthur Hugh Clough –

Father, be my strength, my hope; lift my eyes, O Lord, from my limitedness to Your limitlessness. Amen.

The LORD is my shepherd,
I shall not be in want.
He makes me lie down
in green pastures,
He leads me beside quiet waters,
He restores my soul ...

Even though I walk through
the valley of the shadow of death,
I will fear no evil,
for You are with me;
Your rod and Your staff,
they comfort me.

– PSALM 23:1-4 , NIV –

The other side

"Today shalt thou be with me in paradise."
LUKE 23:43

My library contains a book entitled *Beyond the Shadows*. It was written in about 1880 by an English minister. The unusual dedication on the flyleaf caught my eye: "To the Brotherhood of the Bereaved, to which I belong."

We can see death only from the human point of view. When we have lost someone we love, we are indeed "the bereaved." Jesus, however, has been on the other side of the grave, and all that He has said about death contradicts the traditional ideas of philosophers.

Mankind thinks that death is a great darkness, but, having experienced heaven firsthand, Jesus points out that God sheds eternal light.

We speak of death as a departure; heaven sees it as an arrival.

We call death a hooded spectre; heaven sees it as an angel of light.

We call it separation; heaven calls it reunion.

We call it the grave; heaven calls it the gateway.

We say goodbye here, but it is "Good morning" there.

The sun sets here, but for the Christian, death is indeed "sunrise with Jesus for eternity."

We are bereaved here, but our Christian loved ones bask in the brightness and love of a new life with Jesus.

When you see in the headlines that I am dead, don't you believe it! I'll be alive as never before.

– Dwight L. Moody –

Lord Jesus, still my grief with awareness of the glory which those who are with You enjoy. Amen.

Treasures from clay

In the plain of Jordan did the king cast them [the vessels of the temple,] in the clay ground between Succoth and Zeredathah.

2 CHRONICLES 4:17

When King Solomon was building the great temple in Jerusalem, he used the clay of Succoth to make forms in which to cast the silver, brass, and golden vessels. The clay was dull grey, yellowish, brown, or reddish, having no beauty of its own. Yet it was possible to make a mold from that clay to shape beautiful vessels worthy of a place in the presence of God.

God formed man as a mold of clay capable of shaping a beautiful life. God uses the redeeming work on Calvary and the sanctifying work of the Holy Spirit to purify and refine a surrendered person into the likeness of Jesus Christ. As the apostle Paul expressed it: "But we all, with open face beholding as in a glass the glory of the Lord, are changed into the same image from glory to glory, even as by the Spirit of the Lord" (2 Cor. 3:18).

Thus life is the process in which something beautiful is being shaped by the mold of clay. Death is the blow which shatters that mold to reveal the beautiful life within. This vessel is then transported into the presence of God to worship Him eternally. We do not wonder, then, why the psalmist says, "Precious in the sight of the LORD is the death of His saints" (Ps. 116:15).

If a man has a statue decayed by rust and age, and mutilated in many of its parts, he breaks it up and casts it into a furnace, and after the melting he receives it again in more beautiful form. As thus the dissolving in the furnace was not destruction, but a renewing of the statue; so the death of our bodies is not a destruction, but a renovation.

– John Chrysostom –

Fill my mold, O Lord, with more of Your beauty, and make me a useful vessel in Your kingdom. Amen.

Looking for answers

*For now we see through a glass, darkly; but
then face to face: now I know in part; but
then shall I know even as also I am known.*
1 CORINTHIANS 13:12

One of the hardest confessions for us to make
is, "I don't know." Perhaps our inability to answer
life's deepest questions reminds us of our limitations. If we are honest, we must acknowledge that
man is finite and that there are many things we
would be incapable of understanding even if we
were given the answers.

Someone has said, "I don't know the future,
but I know Him who holds the future." How we
need the security of faith in God! Even though we
do not know the answers to questions like "Why
did this have to happen?" we know the God who
has the answers. And we know that Jesus Christ
Himself is the answer to the most important questions of life.

Individual communion and fellowship with
God's Son is vital. If we want to receive God's gra-

cious gift of forgiveness and life eternal, all we need do is open the door of faith to Jesus Christ. His glorious presence brings us the comfort we need.

In a simple, short conversation with God, you can acknowledge your need and accept the lordship of Jesus Christ. If you do this you will gain permanent friendship with the infinite God, who has all understanding, wisdom, and power. One day you will stand face to face with Jesus Christ, where you shall know even as also you are known by Him. Until that day, you will have the confidence to live without all the answers.

> Not until each loom is silent
> And the shuttles cease to fly,
> Will God unroll the pattern
> And explain the reason why
> The dark threads are as needful
> In the Weaver's skillful hand
> As the threads of gold and silver
> For the pattern which He planned.
> – Anonymous –

Lord Jesus, I am a sinner, poor and weak; You are a Savior, great and strong. Receive me as Your own; I receive You as my God. Amen.

The gardener

"I am the true vine and my Father is the gardener ... Every branch that does bear fruit he trims clean so that it will be even more fruitful."
JOHN 15:1-2

If we pay careful attention to pain, it can instruct and help us. For it sends us to a doctor to find out what is wrong so that we can be healed.

God uses pain and trouble to teach His children important lessons that strengthen character and spiritual life. In His plan difficulties are opportunities for us to grow, but we have to accept the problems in the right spirit.

Jesus tells us that God is the Gardener who prunes us in love. Proper pruning makes vines, bushes, and trees grow better and produce more fruit. Many flowers, such as chrysanthemums, produce larger, more beautiful blossoms when side buds are pinched off. Similarly, we need to have bad habits and wrong thinking pruned away.

God knows where our weaknesses and failures

lie, and He knows the most appropriate times and the best ways to cut them back. If we allow Him to be our Gardener and prune us as He sees fit, He promises that we will be more joyful and more useful in His kingdom. If we trust Him, we can endure the pain as He quietly removes the things that hinder us from bearing more fruit for Him. Through the Gardener's tender care, the wounds He makes are healed.

> Although today He prunes my twigs with pain,
> Yet doth His blood nourish and warm my root:
> Tomorrow I shall put forth buds again
> And clothe myself with fruit.
> – Christina Rosetti –

Father, help me to accept the painful things in my life and concentrate on Your loving and healing presence. Amen.

Grieve, mourn and wail.
Change your laughter
to mourning and your
joy to gloom. Humble
yourselves before the
Lord, and He will lift you up.

– JAMES 4:9-10, NIV –

Before they call I will answer; while they are still speaking I will hear.

— Isaiah 65:24, niv —

The new dimension

O death, where is thy sting? O grave, where is thy victory? The sting of death is sin; and the strength of sin is the law. But thanks be to God, which giveth us the victory through our Lord Jesus Christ.

1 Corinthians 15:55-57

When Jesus rose from the dead, He forever changed our human perspective on death. His victorious return from the grave is proof that death had been vanquished. Man's ancient enemies, sin and death, no longer threaten those who have trusted Jesus Christ as Lord. For Jesus said, "I am the resurrection, and the life: he that believeth in Me, though he were dead, yet shall he live" (John 11:25).

The resurrection of Jesus Christ proves that there is another dimension of life. For He promised, "I go to prepare a place for you. I will come again, and receive you unto myself; that where I am, there ye may be also" (John 14:2-3). This assures us that Jesus Christ will raise all who believe in Him.

Sir Walter Scott said, "Is death the last sleep? No, it is the last and final awakening." Death does not end life; it only changes life from a physical and temporal state to a spiritual and eternal state. Death is the exit by which we leave this life of tragic limitations and enter the Lord's presence.

Let us give thanks to God that our loved ones have entered the new dimension; let us then allow God to meet the needs in our own lives that are created by their absence.

> We picture death as coming to destroy; let us rather picture Christ as coming to save. We think of death as ending; let us rather think of life as beginning, and that more abundantly. We think of losing; let us think of gaining. We think of going away; let us think of arriving. And as the voice of death whispers, "You must go from earth," let us hear the voice of Christ saying, "You are but coming to Me!"
>
> – Norman McLeod –

Father, make real to me the glorious hope of the resurrection. Amen.

The Spirit of fear

For God hath not given us the spirit of fear;
but of power, and of love, and of a sound mind.
2 TIMOTHY 1:7

A talented schoolteacher who was also an active church worker had a large suburban home. Her husband, approaching retirement, was an avid stamp collector with a special room in the house for his valuable collection.

One afternoon she returned from school to find that the house had been broken into; more than ten thousand dollars worth of stamps had been taken. The police said that the thieves must have been professionals who knew about the stamps and that the teacher must have barely missed walking in on them.

From fear of another burglary the couple installed an electronic surveillance system. The house became a fortress – and a prison. When he was hospitalized, she did not dare to stay alone in the house at night. After his death, her mental condition deteriorated. She lived with the poison of fear so long it sapped her life.

Fear can handicap anyone. One of Christ's major ministries was deliverance from the bondage of fear. He often said to His disciples, "Fear not," and He promised them that if they would trust in Him, they would be free indeed.

Only when our faith is focused on God and we remember His power to care for His own can we live in freedom from fear.

Fear not, I am with thee – O be not dismayed.
For I am thy God, I will still give thee aid;
I'll strengthen thee, help thee,
and cause thee to stand,
Upheld by My gracious, omnipotent hand.
– Old Hymn –

In God have I put my trust: I will not be afraid what man can do unto me [Ps. 56:11]. Amen, Lord.

The triumph of patience

I John, who also am your brother, and companion
in tribulation, and in the kingdom and
patience of Jesus Christ, was in the isle that is
called Patmos, for the word of God,
and for the testimony of Jesus Christ.

REVELATION 1:9

We use the term *to be patient* in the sense of "tolerate" – to be able to wait without worrying or fretting. The New Testament Greek word for "to be patient" is derived from two other Greek words, one meaning "under," and the other "to abide." Thus the true meaning of the term is "to remain under" or "to bear."

The apostle John, when exiled on Patmos, said he was "in the patience of Jesus Christ." Patience is a virtue imparted by the Holy Spirit, which enables us to bear up under trials. Sometimes we mistakenly imagine that our faith will exempt us from trials, when actually our faith serves to help us turn trials into triumphs.

Our patience is not resignation to circumstances or to fate. Rather, it is the confidence that, regardless of the situation, our faith will ultimately triumph.

The apostle John, suffering persecution for Christ's sake, was given a vision of the incomparable beauty of heaven. Not only did he see Jesus triumphant, but he saw God's plan for the ages: the ultimate and complete victory of the kingdom of God over all evil. The present sorrow is only a vapor that passes away. The ultimate reward of "the patience of the saints" will be participation in the eternal glory of God.

> There are many trials in life, which do not seem to come from unwisdom or folly; they are silver arrows shot from the bow of God, and fixed inextricably in the quivering heart … They are not meant, like snow or water, to melt as soon as they strike: but the moment an ill can be patiently borne, it is disarmed of its poison, though not of its pain.
> – Henry Ward Beecher –

Keep us in Your patience, O Lord, that we might partake of Your triumph. Amen.

The promises of God

For he hath said, I will never
leave thee, nor forsake thee.
So that we may boldly say,
The Lord is my helper.
HEBREWS 13:5-6

God's promise to us is, "I will never leave thee, nor forsake thee." He repeated this promise four times to different Old Testament characters, and four times He kept His promise.

After Jacob left his parents' home, God spoke to him in a dream, in which Jacob saw angels ascending to and descending from heaven. "Behold, I am with thee," God said, "for I will not leave thee" (Gen. 28:15). And He did not.

When the Israelites were entering the Promised Land, God spoke to Joshua, their leader: "As I was with Moses, so I will be with thee: I will not fail thee, nor forsake thee" (Josh. 1:5). And He did not.

Before King David died, he promised his son and successor, Solomon, that God would enable him to build the great temple: "For the Lord God, even my God, will be with thee: He will not fail thee, nor forsake thee, until thou hast finished all the work" (1 Chron. 28:20). And He did not.

To the prophet Isaiah, when Israel was in great affliction, God said, "Fear thou not; for I am with thee: be not dismayed; for I am thy God" (Isa. 41:10). And He remained with Israel.

In the Book of Hebrews this promise is extended to include all those who trust in Christ. We also may claim it.

> Every divine promise is built upon four pillars: God's justice or holiness, which will not suffer Him to deceive; His grace or goodness, which will not suffer Him to forget; His truth, which will not suffer Him to change; and His power, which makes Him able to accomplish.
>
> – Samuel Salter –

God our Father, help us to claim our legacy: the presence and help of Your Son, our Lord. Amen.

*Cast all your
anxiety on Him
because He
cares for you.*

– 1 PETER 5:7, NIV –

My comfort in my suffering is this: Your promise preserves my life.

— Psalm 119:50, niv —

The birthplace of hope

Why are thou cast down, O my soul?
And why art thou disquieted within me?
Hope in God: for I shall yet praise
him, who is the health of my
countenance, and my God.

As long as we possess hope, we can find strength to go on. But when we have lost those who are closest to us, disappointment and loneliness tempt us to despair. We find it difficult to imagine happiness or purpose ever again returning to our lives. At such times, the Spirit of God says to us lovingly yet sternly, "Hope in God."

Jesus told His disciples, "With God all things are possible" (Matt. 19:26). The greater the need in our lives, the more God longs to fill it. Our deepest needs become channels into which God pours His limitless strength and solace.

The prophet Isaiah wrote, "In the year that King Uzziah died, I saw also the Lord sitting upon a throne" (Isa. 6:1). Sacred communion with God, to an extent the prophet had never experienced before, was born out of his sorrow and fear caused by the death of the king of Judah. In this vision came God's call to Isaiah.

Like Isaiah, you can turn your sorrowing gaze from the past, take your mind off present needs, and hope in God. Your life and the future belong to Him. He still sits upon the throne of the universe, and through His great power and love your life will be renewed. The depths of sorrow in a believing heart can be the birthplace of hope.

Under the storm and the cloud today,
The hard peril and pain –
Tomorrow the stone shall be rolled away,
For the sunshine shall follow the rain.
– Joaquin Miller –

Lord, by Your grace enable this sorrow to be turned to hopeful praise. Amen.

Praying through

Likewise the Spirit also helpeth our infirmities:
for we know not what we should pray for as we
ought: but the Spirit itself maketh intercession for
us with groanings which cannot be uttered. And
he that searcheth the hearts knoweth what is the
mind of the Spirit, because he maketh intercession
for the saints according to the will of God.
ROMANS 8:26-27

When we most need to pray, we feel least capable of praying. It is difficult to pray confidently when our heart is heavy with grief. But, praise be to God, answered prayer is due not to the completeness of our prayer, but to the goodness of Him who hears. We may not think that our weeping heart can pray effectively, but does a shiny key open a lock better than a tarnished one?

It is not how much or how well we pray, but simply that we pray. Prayer in the "valley of the shadow of death" confirms that the Shepherd is indeed with us.

Jesus said, "Ask, and it shall be given you" (Luke

11:9). Simply whisper a prayer for comfort, for strength, for wisdom, for rest, for peace, and you will feel the Master's touch. His "rod and staff" will comfort you and enable you to pass through the dark shadows and come once again into the light.

You do not pray alone. The Holy Spirit intercedes for you with wisdom of which you are not capable. When you are confused and uncertain of God's leading, the Spirit prays for you "according to the will of God." You can never know the full sufficiency of God's provision until you reach your own limits. Where your prayers stop, the Holy Spirit's start. God asks only that you turn your heart toward Him.

> Prayer is not overcoming God's reluctance;
> it is laying hold of His highest willingness.
> – Richard Chenevix Trench –

Lord, teach us to pray our way through the dark valley into the light of Your everlasting day. Amen.

Special delivery

And the LORD came, and stood, and called as at other times, Samuel, Samuel. Then Samuel answered, Speak; for thy servant heareth.

1 SAMUEL 3:10

Two women were discussing the sermon they had just heard, and found that each had been impressed by something different. In each case it was not the theme of the sermon that left an imprint but a remark in passing or an illustration.

Psychologists call this "selective attention." We tune in to that part of a message that speaks to our special needs and interests. Even the message we get from reading the Bible is determined as much by our own views and concerns as by the words we read. Someone has said that we see things not as they are but as we are.

Why? Because God made each of us to be as unique as our fingerprints. Even brothers and sisters are different. And the longer we live, the more distinct our personalities become. God knows you and me individually and He knows just what our needs are.

God makes His messages applicable to each individual. He speaks to each of us about Himself and His will in "private language" – the language that will be meaningful to the individual. God sees that His message is coded to each person's background and experience. If we listen prayerfully – "Speak; for thy servant heareth" – He will get through to us with the message that meets our particular need.

> True prayer never comes weeping home: I am sure that I shall get either what I ask, or what I ought to have asked.
> – Robert Leighton –

O Lord, speak to me in a way that I can understand, and inspire me to do Your will. Amen.

The end of mourning

And, behold, there came a great wind from the wilderness, and smote the four corners of the house, and it fell upon the young men, and they are dead … Then Job arose, and rent his mantle, and shaved his head, and fell down upon the ground, and worshipped, And said, … the LORD gave, and the LORD hath taken away; blessed be the name of the LORD.

JOB 1:19-21

The season of mourning must end lest it become a perpetual winter to our souls. Sorrow must give way to worship, which brings reviving joy, a clearer vision of God, and a brighter outlook on life.

At the news of his children's deaths, Job went through the process of grief. First he tore his clothes. This reflected his initial shock and dismay, which is normal and natural in the human experience.

Then Job shaved his head. This symbolized Job's honor of those who had died, but also humility before God. Even at this time of great grief, Job kept his life submitted to God.

Last, Job fell down and worshipped. Worship is the action by which we focus our whole beings on God that we might consider His greatness and holiness – who He is and what He does. Job rose from this worship with praise on his lips: "Blessed be the name of the LORD." By entering the presence of the Lord in worship, Job's spirit had been revived and his soul restored.

Worship is the final resolution of our grief and mourning. Let us worship God that we might know Him who transcends our troubled lives, that we might gain new perspective and understanding for living, and that we might always witness with praise for Him who is our Redeemer.

> Worship liberates the personality by giving a new perspective to life, by integrating life with the multitude of life-forms, by bringing into the life the virtues of humility, loyalty, devotion and rightness of attitude, thus refreshing and reviving the spirit.
>
> – Roswell C. Long –

Father, open my eyes that I might worship Thee; open my heart that I might love Thee; open my lips that I might praise Thee. Amen.

Where, O death, is your victory?
Where, O death, is your sting?
The sting of death is sin,
and the power of sin is the law.
But thanks be to God!
He gives us the victory through
our Lord Jesus Christ.

– 1 Corinthians 15:55-57, niv –

The eyes of the LORD are
on the righteous and His ears
are attentive to their cry.

– PSALM 34:15, NIV –

Courage

O love the LORD, all ye his saints: for the LORD preserveth the faithful, and plentifully rewardeth the proud doer. Be of good courage, and he shall strengthen your heart, all ye that hope in the LORD.
PSALM 31:23-24

Nothing threatens our courage more than the loss of loved ones. Yet that is the time we most need our courage: courage to go on, when we would rather look back; courage to be strong, when we are most aware of our weakness; courage to reach out to others, when we would rather retreat into solitude; courage to make decisions for tomorrow, when we still are concerned with yesterday. Death has taken enough already; let us not reward this vile thief by permitting him to kill our courage as well.

Courage is derived from two sources: confidence in one's resources, and belief in the value of one's purpose. God provides both the strength and the purpose of the believer; thus we should be of infinite courage.

Fear and resignation reinforce cowardice, but our faith and perseverance will give us victory over it. Adoniram Judson, the great missionary to Burma, wrote,

> In spite of sorrow, loss, and pain,
> Our courage be onward still;
> We sow on Burma's barren plain,
> We reap on Zion's hill.

When we have the perspective of faith we peer beyond time into eternity. Then we see that death was a mere milepost to our loved ones who are now in God's loving embrace. Our courage will grow strong as we take hold of God's promises.

> Take courage. It is sweet to talk with God; we walk in the wilderness today and in the promised land tomorrow.
> – Dwight L. Moody –

Father, renew my courage, calm my fears, and let me be resolute in You. Amen.

Faith's reward

*For I know that my redeemer liveth, and that he
shall stand at the latter day upon the earth: And
though after my skin worms destroy this body, yet
in my flesh shall I see God; Whom I shall see for
myself, and mine eyes shall behold, and not
another; though my reins be consumed within me.*

JOB 19:25-27

In affliction and distress, we can look to ourselves, focus on the circumstances, or turn to God.
If we look to ourselves, we see the limits of our
own resources and chastise ourselves for our faults
and failures; the result is self-condemnation. If we
focus on the circumstances, we realize our help-
lessness to change them; the result is despair. But
if we turn to God, we see One who in all circumstances is greater than we are; the result is faith.

Faith is knowing the God who holds the future
and putting our hand in His. The person who has
faith does not have all the answers, but he knows
Someone who does. Although faith does not enable us to see specific events in the future, it allows

us to see many things about God we would not see otherwise.

We see, first, God's benevolence toward us, which ensures that all tragedy will turn to triumph in the end. Second, we see that God is just. Therefore, all the evils, injustices, and pains of this world are temporary and will give way to the permanent peace of His everlasting kingdom. And third, faith enables us to see God as our Provider who will meet "all [our] need according to His riches in glory" (Phil. 4:19). He is able to care for us in all circumstances. Through our faith, we see God's hand in everything. The results of faith are immediate and the rewards are ultimate.

> Unbelief starves the soul; faith finds food in famine, and a table in the wilderness. In the greatest danger; faith says, "I have a great God." When outward strength is broken, faith rests on the promises. In the midst of sorrow, faith draws the sting out of every trouble, and takes out the bitterness from every affliction.
> – Robert Cecil –

Father, I place my faith in You. Reveal Yourself to me. Amen.

Casting out fear

*Behold, God is my salvation; I will trust, and
not be afraid: for the LORD Jehovah is my strength
and my song: He also is become my salvation.*

ISAIAH 12:2

Throughout the Bible we hear God telling His
people to cast out fear. Repeatedly He says to His
chosen leaders, "Fear not!"

When the Egyptian army had pursued the
fleeing Israelites to the Red Sea, God ordered His
people, "Fear ye not, stand still, and see the salvation of the LORD." After they obeyed, God commanded Moses, "Speak unto the children of Israel,
that they go forward" (Exod. 14:13-15).

After Moses' death, God encouraged Joshua
with these words: "Be strong and of a good courage; be not afraid, neither be thou dismayed"
(Josh. 1:9).

Later God spoke similar words to Gideon, a
leader of Israel's army. God repeated them to Isaiah, Jeremiah, Daniel, and others, and through
many prophets to the nation Israel.

In the New Testament, Christ often said, "Fear not." When His disciples' boat was about to be swamped, He came to them and said, "It is I; be not afraid" (John 6:20). When at the Last Supper He spoke of the future, He comforted them with the words, "Let not your heart be troubled, neither let it be afraid" (John 14:27).

Today, in times of distress and sorrow and anxiety, God still says, "Fear not." We must not let fear paralyze us. With faith in the Lord, we too can overcome fear and move forward.

> Our doubts are traitors,
> And make us lose the good we oft might win
> By fearing to attempt.
> – William Shakespeare –

O Lord, in times of difficulty, give me the courage and common sense to turn away from my fears and reach out my hand to You. Amen.

Trust in God

*Trust in the LORD, and do good; so shalt
thou dwell in the land, and verily thou shalt
be fed ... Commit thy way unto the LORD;
trust also in him, and he shall bring it
to pass. And he shall bring forth thy
righteousness as the light, and
thy judgment as the noonday. Rest in
the LORD, and wait patiently for him ...*
PSALM 37:3, 5-7

Trust is quiet confidence we place in someone
we love. The Word of God instructs us again and
again to place our trust in God. The greater the
burden we bear, the greater is our need simply to
trust the Lord. He never ceases to have our good
in mind. His purpose, always, is to provide for our
needs and to help us obey His will. The fact that
we do not know how He intends to do this does
not mean we cannot trust Him, for God makes
no mistakes.

John Macduff has said, "Trust God where you
cannot trace Him. Do not try to penetrate the

cloud He brings over you; rather look to the bow that is on it. The mystery is God's; the promise is yours."

Even though we do not fully understand the surgery our doctor recommends, we still trust the surgeon. We may know nothing of aerodynamics and airplanes, yet we still enjoy the convenience of flying. One of the things that make sorrow so difficult for us is our inability to understand what has happened to us and what will happen next. Yet at times like this, our trust in God brings us much needed peace and the privilege of watching God "bring it to pass." When you "rest in the Lord, and wait patiently for Him," your sorrow will turn to praise.

Look at that beautiful bird, and learn from it to trust in God. One might wonder where it could live in tempestuous nights, in the whirlwind, or in the stormy day; but I have noticed it is safe and dry under the broad leaf while rivers have been flooded, and the mountain oaks torn up from their roots.

Lord, I give myself and all my problems to You in the confidence that You do all things well. Amen.

Think not thou canst sigh a sigh,
And thy Maker is not by;
Think not thou canst weep a tear,
And thy Maker is not near.

Cast your cares on the LORD
and He will sustain you;
He will never let the righteous fall.

– PSALM 55:22, NIV –

Self-protection

*Every word of God is pure: he is a shield
unto them that put their trust in him.*
PROVERBS 30:5

An experienced police officer, who had never
been shot at in his thirteen years on the force,
nevertheless always wore a bulletproof vest. One
day he was shot in the back by an unseen foe. The
vest saved his life; he suffered only a bruise.

"As long as my badge is showing," he said, "I
know I'm always a target – so I wear the vest."

The "shield of faith" that the apostle Paul, in
Ephesians 6:16, urges all Christians to wear is like
a bulletproof vest. Because we belong to Christ,
we are always under attack by Satan. He tries to
destroy us by doubt, despair, and temptation to
sin. And when trouble comes – when we have illness or difficulty, when we feel like asking God
"why?" or when grief overwhelms us – we are especially easy prey to Satan's wiles.

Like the police officer, we need to be aware
that, because we wear the badge of Christ, we will

be a target for Satan. Constant, close communication with God will serve as a bulletproof vest, assuring us of His protection.

> We rest on Thee – our Shield and our Defender!
> We go not forth alone against the foe:
> Strong in Thy strength,
> Safe in Thy keeping tender,
> We rest on Thee, and in Thy Name we go.
> – Edith G. Cherry –

O Lord, when I am weakened by doubt or trouble, shield and comfort me. Amen.

A widow's faith

*That your faith – of greater worth
than gold which perishes even though
refined by fire – may be proved genuine
and may result in praise, glory and
honor when Jesus Christ is revealed.*
1 PETER 1:7 (ASV)

Elijah had informed Ahab that because of his wickedness no rain would fall on the land. Then the word of the Lord came to Elijah and warned him to hide. So Elijah went to live by the brook Cherith. Later, the brook dried up. Then the Lord told Elijah to go to the village of Zarephath. "Behold, I have commanded a widow there to sustain thee."

Severe drought and famine prevailed over all the land, and the widow did not have much to share; she used the last of her provisions to cook a meal for the prophet. Miraculously, "the barrel of meal was not used up, neither did the cruse of oil fail, according to the word of the LORD" (1 Kings 17:8-16).

After a while, the widow's son died. Then the power of God enabled Elijah to revive the child.

Like Elijah and the widow, we can never know when we will be severely tested, but we can take courage from the knowledge that God will sustain us, perhaps in unexpected ways. God met the widow's needs daily in the small necessities of life and also through a great miracle. He will be with us and choose the best way to meet our problems.

If God gives faith He will surely try it, and if He leads us out into service and testimony for Him, He will surely try us and prove how far we are depending upon Him alone.
– J. R. Caldwell –

Heavenly Father, when I am heartsick, remind me that my faith in You not only lifts me up but honors Your name. Amen.

Working together

*And we know that all things work together
for good to them that love God, to them who
are the called according to his purpose.*

ROMANS 8:28

When trials come, we find it difficult to believe
that God can and does work all things together for
our good. But however little we may have left in
our life, that is enough for God to carry out His
eternal purposes for us. We never lose so much
that God does not have something with which He
can work out good in our life.

God is much greater than we can understand.
His power is unlimited and His love unending –
how can we comprehend His purpose?

God wants us to ask for and expect His inter-
vention in our life. After great grief, it may seem
out of place to speak of God's working this out
for our good, but that is part of our comfort and
healing. If we have no hope in the future, we have
inadequate strength for today. Tomorrow's hopes
are today's incentives. To those who love God, the

greatest incentive is knowing that good will be worked out for us. Quiet trust and confidence in God release His power for our good.

How then do we learn to trust more? Phillips Brooks said it well: "We trust as we love and where we love. If we love Christ much; surely we shall trust Him much." If we love Him, good is always to be expected.

I will not doubt though all my ships at sea
Come drifting home with broken masts and sails:
I will believe the Hand which never fails.
From seeming evil worketh good for me;
And though I weep because those sails are tattered,
Still will I cry, while my best hopes lie shattered –
"I trust in Thee!"
– Elle Wheeler Wilcox –

Father, thank You for Your promise of working all things together for our good. In this we will love and trust You, today as we can, tomorrow more. Amen.

Thankfulness

Be careful for nothing; but in every thing by prayer and supplication with thanksgiving let your requests be made known unto God. And the peace of God, which passeth all understanding, shall keep your hearts and minds through Christ Jesus.

PHILIPPIANS 4:6-7

All too often we seem to be thankful only when we experience kindness and fair weather. It is not common for us to thank God during a violent rainstorm, nor is it common for someone in grief to have a thankful heart. Yet the apostle Paul says, "In every thing give thanks: for this is the will of God in Christ Jesus concerning you" (1 Thess. 5:18).

Notice that this verse does not admonish us to give thanks *for* everything. God does not expect us to be thankful for things like death, darkness, or disease. The important thing is that we focus on the goodness of God, the thoughtfulness of other people, and the many blessings, which remain to us.

"The LORD gave, and the LORD hath taken

away," wrote Job, "blessed be the name of the LORD" (1:21b). This is what he said after he was told of the tragedies that had befallen his family and possessions. Job fell down and worshiped God; not even sorrow could dissuade him from an offering of thankfulness. Let us not forget that the Lord who "taketh away" also gives to us again. Our losses can never outnumber our gains; therefore our thankfulness should always exceed our sorrow.

The result of thankful worship is "peace that passes understanding." How our hearts are settled when we offer thanks! We need often to show our gratitude for God's provision and faithfulness.

> When you have truly thanked the Lord
> For every blessing sent,
> But little time will then remain
> For murmur and lament.
>
> – Anonymous –

O Lord, thank You that Your provision always exceeds our needs. Amen.

*For the LORD comforts His
people and will have
compassion on His afflicted ones.*

– ISAIAH 49:13B, NIV –

The righteous cry out,
and the LORD hears them;
He delivers them from
all their troubles.
The LORD is close to
the brokenhearted
and saves those who
are crushed in spirit.

– PSALM 34:17-18, NIV –

The triumph of faith

Behold, I have refined thee, but not with silver;
I have chosen thee in the furnace of affliction.
ISAIAH 48:10

Can any good come of sorrow? Yes. Now we are short-sighted: we can see only pain, suffering, and loneliness. We wonder what will fill the empty spot, what will soothe the aching heart. But life will go on and slowly the tunnel vision of today will give way to expanded horizons. Thus it is wise for us to consider how the greatest good can come of this.

Out of the experience of sorrow can arise hope and inspiration. You will find that sorrow has made you more sympathetic to the needs of others. Perhaps because of this encounter with death you will find a new appreciation of life. From the loss of someone you love you will learn to draw closer to those who yet remain. You may be called on to complete the unfinished task begun by one whose life was cut short. Through all this you will be enriched and able to contribute more in the years that remain.

Reach out now in faith to receive God's therapy. There are two things that fling light into the darkness of death: the triumph of faith that permeates present life and the assurance of resurrection that defeats death. Both are from the Lord.

> No words can express how much the world owes to sorrow. Most of the Psalms were born in the wilderness. Most of the epistles were written in prison … In bonds Bunyan lived the allegory that he afterwards indited, and we may thank Bedford Jail for the "Pilgrims' Progress." Take comfort, afflicted Christian! When God is about to make pre-eminent use of a man, He puts him in the fire.
>
> – George Macdonald –

Lord, help me to recover from the sorrow of death and help me to find greater meaning in life. Amen.

Time of growth

*Sorrow is better than laughter: for by the sadness
of the countenance the heart is made better.*

ECCLESIASTES 7:3

At the first news of a miracle worker called Jesus,
many people echoed an old saying: "Can there any
good thing come out of Nazareth?" The Nazarenes
were a simple people; few of them were educated
and their speech was rough. Yet from Nazareth
came our Savior.

In much the same way we glibly ask, "Can any
good come from sorrow?" Yet King Solomon, a
wise man who wrote three great books of the Old
Testament, said that "sorrow is better than laughter." This was not an idle remark, but was inspired
by the Holy Spirit.

Sorrow can be valuable – that is an eternal
truth. It is often the forerunner of a closer, dearer
fellowship with God. Frequently, those who have
suffered most know God best. Why? Because the
Savior's compassion draws Him to those with the
greatest need. In fact, Jesus was often criticized for

spending time with publicans, harlots, and lepers. Today, likewise, through His dedicated followers Jesus gently ministers to the afflicted. Sorrow brings us nearer to Him and purifies us. Indeed, sorrow is a fire to consume our vices, a soothing rain to give growth to our virtues.

> Sorrow is our John the Baptist, clad in grim garments, with rough arms, a son of the wilderness, baptizing us with bitter tears, preaching repentance; and behind him comes the gracious, affectionate, healing Lord, speaking peace and joy to the soul.
>
> – Frederic D. Huntington –

Lord, magnify Your presence in the midst of my grief. Amen.

Let him go

*I know that, whatsoever God doeth,
it shall be for ever ...
That which hath been is now;
and that which is to be
hath already been; and
God requireth that which is past.*

ECCLESIASTES 3:14-15

Loose him, and let him go," Jesus said to the friends of Lazarus (John 11:44). Lazarus was loosed to go back to his earthly life, but those of us who have lost loved ones in death need to loose them to their new and eternal life with Christ. This is one of the most difficult things in all the world – the past is yet so vivid and eternity is beyond our imagination.

A young widow who had moved with her children to a distant city to be nearer her family was befriended by an older widow. As time passed, the younger woman continued to dwell on her memories. Her friend pointed out a passage from the prophet Isaiah: "Forget the former things;

don not dwell on the past. See, I am doing a new thing! Now it springs up; do you not percieve it?" (43:18-19, NIV).

God requires that we relinquish the past to Him and march forward. Even good things and happy times, if we cling to them and try to relive them, can hinder our growth. When we release our loved one to God, He can open up to us His perfect will for our future.

> "He is near the land of the dying," whispered those by the bedside of an old Scottish preacher. Overhearing them, he answered, "Nay! I'm now in the land of the dying; I am near the land of the living!"
> – Anonymous –

Lord Jesus, help me to live the best I can in the present and look forward to the future You have in store for me. Amen.

Growing pains

*My brethren, count it all joy when you
fall into diverse temptations; knowing
this, that the trying of your faith
worketh patience. But let patience
have her perfect work, that ye may be
perfect and entire, wanting nothing ...
Blessed is the man that endureth temptation:
for when he is tried, he shall receive the
crown of life, which the Lord hath
promised to them that love him.*
JAMES 1:2-4, 12

The fire that consumes coal purifies gold. Both
are minerals from the earth, but gold has certain
properties, lacking in coal, that make it valuable.
Gold can withstand high temperatures; it is mal-
leable and can be formed easily; it is glossy and
reflects the light.

There is also a difference in the reactions of
people who are subjected to trials. Those who
trust the Lord are purified by their trials and gain
strength from them, while those who distrust God

are consumed by their bitterness and cynicism. For those who trust God, tribulations can bring completion, character, and triumph. For those who doubt, difficulty and trial lead to confusion, depression, and destruction.

How are you reacting to your tragedy and misfortune? Do you blame God and pull away from Him, or do you draw closer and look to Him for comfort, wisdom, and understanding? When we shoot arrows of anger, frustration, and bitterness at God, they simply fall back on our own heads. But when we seek Him in prayer and worship, His blessings shower on us.

When James says, "count it all joy," he means that we should have an inner confidence in God, expecting divine help and comfort. For those who trust God, trials are times of growing to new levels of character and maturity.

> Tribulation will not hurt you, ... unless it hardens you, and makes you sour and narrow and skeptical.
> – Edwin H. Chapin –

Lord, may the testing fires of this life draw me closer to You and bring more of Your fullness to me. Amen.

The LORD *is good, a refuge
in times of trouble. He cares
for those who trust in Him.*

– NAHUM 1:7, NIV –

Come to Me, all you who
are weary and burdened,
and I will give you rest.

– MATTHEW 11:28, NIV –

Beyond the horizon

*But without faith it is impossible to
please him: for he that cometh to God
must believe that he is, and that he is a
rewarder of them that diligently seek him.*
HEBREWS 11:6

When Columbus set sail for America, one part of his experience that we rarely consider is the long stretch of days when he was aware that he and his men had passed the point of no return and faced possible starvation. As the supplies were running out and his men were becoming mutinous, Columbus said, "Sail on!" What a tremendous faith he exercised in what lay beyond the horizon!

Today we need that kind of "sail-on" faith. A persistent faith helps us to face immediate problems and to trust that God will guide us in the future.

The invincible God must be the object of our faith. Our God parted the Red Sea and raised the dead. He loved us enough to give His Son to die for our sins and reconcile us to Himself. He is concerned about each of us, having numbered every hair on our heads, and watching over the lowliest creatures, even the sparrows.

God is a Spirit and we cannot see Him. Yet we can believe His Word that He will sustain us through life's trials. Trusting His love and His care, we can sail safely through unknown waters to a new land whose beauty and happiness are grander than our highest dreams.

> Faith is the daring of the soul to go farther than it can see.
> – William Newton Clarke –

Thank You, Lord God, for rewarding us when we diligently seek You. Help us to trust You more completely. Amen.

Toward sunrise

Weeping may endure for a night,
but joy cometh in the morning.
PSALM 30:5

The Book of Genesis tells us that when God created the earth, "the evening and the morning were the first day." Since then, every evening has been followed by a morning. God's master plan of the ages ends with an eternal morning – the light of God's presence will never fail.

In the Bible, death is often expressed as "falling asleep" – with the implied hope of waking to a resurrection morning. "David slept with his fathers," we read in 1 Kings 2:10. We note also that when Jesus died on the cross, "the graves were opened; and many bodies of the saints which slept arose" (Matt. 27:52).

When we suffer loss, we weep and find it hard to believe that sunrise will come again to dispel the darkness we feel. Yet the Bible is full of assurances that night will pass and dawn will come again. At the end of the Bible, Jesus says of Himself: "I am the root and the offspring of David, and the bright and morning star" (Rev. 22:16).

> Hope child, tomorrow and tomorrow still,
> And every morrow hope; trust while you live.
> Hope, each time the dawn doth fill,
> Be there to ask as God is there to give.
> – Victor Hugo –

Lord Jesus, thank You for Your assurance that the sun will again shine, and that it will shine eternally. Amen.

The flag of joy

Rejoice in the Lord always; and again I say, Rejoice.
PHILIPPIANS 4:4

Ye shall be called the children of the Highest," Jesus said (Luke 6:35). "Ye are My friends … I have chosen you" (John 15:14-16). "These things have I spoken unto you … that your joy might be full" (John 15:11). Such positive statements were often on His lips, Jesus Himself will replace our sorrow with joy that no one can take from us.

The Lord knows that we are weak, sinful, needy, and helpless, but He never dwells on these things because He is the Great Physician who offers an everlasting cure. He says that He has made us heirs of God in eternity: "Because I live, ye shall live also" (John 14:19). The freedom provided by Christ results in an inner fountain of joy.

How do we display this flag of joy? We celebrate the reality of Jesus' birth. His death on the cross, and His resurrection. We keep His commandments.

We speak often of Him. Like the apostle Paul,

we love to proclaim God's Word and rejoice over those who accept it.

Genuine joy in the Lord witnesses more effectively than many sermons. When the peace and joy Jesus gives dwell in the human heart, eternal life and love shine through the personality. Then people notice and say, "Whatever you've got, I want it!"

> Joy is the flag flying from the battlement of the Christian heart to show that the King is in residence.
> – James S. Stewart –

Lord Jesus, let me rejoice in Your presence and radiate Your love. Amen.

Pass it on

*Blessed be God, even the Father of our Lord
Jesus Christ, the Father of mercies, and the God
of all comfort; Who comforteth us in all our
tribulation that we may be able to comfort
them which are in any trouble, by the comfort
wherewith we ourselves are comforted of God.*

2 Corinthians 1:3-4

The sorrows of the faithful weave a heavenly beauty into their lives. For the Word of God promises us that all things, even sorrows will work together for our good. In our darkest valleys, we may discover some of our brightest treasures.

Only the apostle Paul uses the expression "the God of all comfort." Through his many afflictions, Paul had learned this important truth: God can comfort everyone in everything. God is rich in mercy and will faithfully comfort us "in all our tribulation." As Thomas Moore said, "Earth has no sorrows that heaven cannot heal."

Yet the comfort we receive is only the immediate reward of our communion with God. God's comfort continues to pay dividends, for we are enabled thereby to comfort others. Indeed, many times our own sorrow melts as we minister to someone else in his or her need. Our hearts are made sensitive to others by the trials we have gone through ourselves. Our part of God's work is to express His love through human helpfulness.

What comfort you receive, give lovingly to someone else. There is nothing in God's economy that will not increase when it is shared or given away.

> The happiest, sweetest, tenderest homes are not those where there has been no sorrow, but those, which have been overshadowed with grief, and where Christ's comfort was accepted. The very memory of the sorrow is a gentle benediction that broods ever over the household, like the silence that comes after prayer. There is a blessing sent from God in every burden of sorrow.
> – James R. Miller –

God of all comfort, comfort us still with Your healing balm, and help us learn to be as gentle with our touch as You are with Yours. Amen.

*H*e heals the brokenhearted,
and binds up their wounds.

– PSALM 147:3, NIV –

... and surely I am
with you always,
to the very end of the age.

– MATTHEW 28:20, NIV –

The right to tears

And God shall wipe away all tears from their eyes; and there shall be no more death, neither sorrow, nor crying, neither shall there be any more pain: for the former things are passed away.

REVELATION 21:4

A widow apologized to the group for her tearfulness, "It's been more than a year since Bill's death," she said. "I know I should be over all this, but when I came into church, two couples to whom we had been close were sitting in our usual pew. Suddenly I couldn't stand it that Bill wasn't here so that we could go sit with them again."

Tears of grief are nothing to be ashamed of. They are a human response to bereavement and often serve as a safety valve for our emotions. The New Testament tells us that "Jesus wept" with the family of Lazarus (John 11:35).

In the quiet sanctuary of our souls, however, we sometimes need to ask ourselves, for whom do we weep? Mostly, we weep for our own unbearable loneliness – because we are separated from our loved ones, because we hurt.

As we make necessary adjustments to life, it is inevitable that we will weep. The Bible does not tell us that we should not weep, only that Christians, in their sorrow, should not be even as others which have not hope" (1 Thess. 4:13). Faith shining through our grief causes the rest of the world to marvel.

> The soul would have no rainbow had the eyes no tears.
> – John Vance Cheney –

Lord, help me to let Your love and joy form a rainbow through my tears. Amen.

A time for singing

Turn again our captivity, O LORD, as the streams in the south. They that sow in tears shall reap in joy. He that goeth forth and weepeth, bearing precious seed, shall doubtless come again with rejoicing, bringing his sheaves with him.

PSALM 126:4-6

Our wise God and Father has varied the times of our life even as He varies the seasons. The time of sorrow seems to stretch out to infinity. Sorrow always insists that she has come to stay, but we should not believe her. Now we suffer sorrow and grief, but we will again experience joy and singing. Unless we stubbornly cling to sorrow, its season will pass.

King Solomon said, "To every thing there is a season, and a time to every purpose under the heaven: A time to be born, and a time to die; … A time to weep, and a time to laugh; a time to mourn, and a time to dance" (Eccles. 3:1-2, 4).

The psalmist knew this inevitability of God's renewing and restoring mercies. Unless we simply refuse to be comforted, God will always alleviate our sorrows with His joy. The darkest night in history still had a dawn; the worst storm of all ages was followed by a calm. For the Christian, the pain of this world will be followed by paradise.

As you partake of the Lord's comfort, a song will begin to rise again in your heart. This time it will ring with a deeper, richer melody, more certain in hope, more complete with joy. Like birds, we sing best after our cages have been darkened for a while.

> Out of suffering have emerged the strongest souls; the most massive characters are seamed with scars. Martyrs have put on their coronation robes glittering with fire, and through their tears have the sorrowful first seen the gates of heaven.
> – Edwin H. Chapin –

Lord, free us from our captivity to depression. Let our sorrow turn to joy, our weeping to Your praise. Amen.

*P*raise be to the
God and Father
of our Lord Jesus
Christ, the Father
of compassion and
the God of all comfort,
who comforts us
in all our troubles,
so that we can
comfort those in any
trouble with the
comfort we ourselves
have received from God.

– 2 CORINTHIANS 1:3-4, NIV –

Do not be anxious about anything, but in everything, by prayer and petition, with thanksgiving, present your requests to God. And the peace of God, which transcends all understanding, will guard your hearts and your minds in Christ Jesus.

— PHILIPPIANS 4:6-7, NIV —

The ransomed of
the LORD will return,
they will enter Zion
with singing;
everlasting joy will
crown their heads.
Gladness and joy
will overtake them,
and sorrow and
sighing will flee away.

– ISAIAH 51:11, NIV –